Survival Essentials

Must-Know Techniques for Wilderness and Urban
Survival

Samson Kennedy

1

Must-Know Techniques for Wilderness and Urban
Survival

Survival Essentials

TABLE OF CONTENTS

Chapter 1: Introduction

The Importance of Survival Skills

Survival skills are the foundation upon which human resilience and adaptability are built. These skills ensure that one can navigate the challenges posed by both natural and urban environments, turning potentially life-threatening situations into manageable ones. The importance of survival skills cannot be overstated, as they empower individuals to face emergencies with confidence and resourcefulness.

Understanding the essence of survival skills begins with recognizing their historical significance. For centuries, our ancestors relied on these abilities to hunt, gather, build shelters, and navigate through wilderness. These skills were passed down through generations, forming the bedrock of human civilization. Today, while the context may have changed, the need for survival skills remains as pertinent as ever. Natural disasters, unexpected accidents, and sudden societal disruptions can thrust anyone into scenarios where these skills become critical.

In modern society, the dependency on technology and infrastructure has created a false sense of security. Many people assume that emergency services will always be available, or that their daily environment will remain stable. However, history has shown that disruptions can occur suddenly and without warning. Earthquakes, floods, hurricanes, and even urban crises like power outages or civil unrest can leave individuals stranded and self-reliant. In these moments, having a well-rounded set of survival skills can make the difference between life and death.

Mental resilience is a cornerstone of effective survival. The ability to remain calm, focused, and decisive in high-stress situations is critical. Panic can cloud judgment, leading to poor decisions that exacerbate already dire circumstances. Developing mental resilience involves training oneself to handle stress through controlled exposure to challenging scenarios. Techniques such as mindfulness meditation, controlled breathing, and visualization exercises can help build this resilience. Practicing these techniques regularly can ensure that when a real-life emergency arises, the mind remains clear and capable of rational thought.

Situational awareness is another vital component of survival skills. This involves being acutely aware of one's surroundings and understanding the potential threats and resources available. In urban environments, situational awareness means noticing exits, identifying safe zones, and being aware of the people around you. In wilderness settings, it involves understanding the terrain, weather patterns, and the presence of wildlife. Cultivating situational awareness can be achieved through simple daily practices, such as observing details in familiar environments or periodically pausing to assess your surroundings during routine activities.

Decision-making in survival scenarios often requires quick thinking and prioritization. The acronym S.T.O.P.—Stop, Think, Observe, and Plan—serves as a useful guide. When faced with a crisis, the first step is to stop and avoid immediate action driven by panic. Taking a moment to think allows for the assessment of the situation. Observing the environment helps in identifying resources and potential threats. Finally, planning involves devising a course of action based on the observations made. This systematic approach ensures that decisions are made logically rather than impulsively.

Water is essential for survival, and knowing how to find and purify it is crucial. In the wilderness, natural water sources such as streams and lakes can be invaluable, but they often contain harmful pathogens. Techniques such as boiling water, using portable water filters, or employing chemical purification tablets can make water safe to drink. In urban settings, locating water might involve knowing where public water sources are or understanding how to harvest rainwater safely. Keeping a supply of water purification tools in an emergency kit can be a lifesaver.

Fire is another fundamental element of survival. It provides warmth, protection, and the means to cook food and purify water. Learning various fire-starting techniques, such as using flint and steel, friction methods like bow drills, or even modern tools like lighters and fire starters, is invaluable. Practicing these methods in different conditions, such as wet or windy environments, ensures that one can reliably create fire when needed.

Shelter is critical in both wilderness and urban survival scenarios. Exposure to the elements can quickly lead to hypothermia or heatstroke, making it imperative to have a plan for shelter. In the wilderness, this might involve building a lean-to, debris hut, or snow cave. Understanding how to use natural materials effectively can provide insulation and protection. In urban environments, seeking out structurally sound buildings, creating makeshift shelters from available materials, or even understanding how to safely use an abandoned vehicle for refuge can provide necessary protection.

Food, while less immediately critical than water or shelter, is still an important aspect of survival. In wilderness settings, knowledge of edible plants, foraging techniques, and basic hunting and trapping can provide sustenance. Understanding which plants are safe to eat and how to prepare them is essential to avoid poisoning. In urban areas, knowing where to find food in stores, understanding how to safely scavenge, and having basic knowledge of urban foraging can be crucial. Keeping a stockpile of non-perishable food items in an emergency kit can also provide a reliable food source during initial stages of a crisis.

First aid skills are indispensable in survival situations. The ability to treat wounds, manage infections, and handle common injuries can prevent minor issues from becoming life-threatening. Basic first aid knowledge includes understanding how to clean and dress wounds, perform CPR, treat burns, and manage fractures. Having a well-stocked first aid kit and knowing how to use each item within it can significantly increase chances of survival.

Communication plays a pivotal role in survival, particularly in urban settings where staying informed can dictate the course of action. Knowing how to use radios, understanding emergency broadcast signals, and having a plan for contacting loved ones can provide critical information and support. In the wilderness, signaling for rescue using mirrors, whistles, or creating visible markers can attract attention from rescuers.

Ultimately, the will to survive is perhaps the most critical survival skill of all. This intrinsic drive motivates individuals to push through hardships and overcome obstacles. Stories of survival often highlight this unyielding determination. Cultivating a positive mindset, setting small, achievable goals, and maintaining hope can fuel the will to survive even in the direst circumstances.

In conclusion, survival skills encompass a broad range of knowledge and abilities that empower individuals to face emergencies with confidence and resourcefulness. These skills, rooted in our ancestors' practices, remain crucial in today's world. By developing mental resilience, situational awareness, decision-making abilities, and practical skills such as water purification, fire starting, shelter building, food foraging, first aid, and communication, individuals can navigate and overcome the challenges posed by both wilderness and urban environments. The importance of these skills cannot be overstated, as they are the tools that ensure survival in the face of adversity.

Survival skills encompass a vast range of knowledge and techniques that prepare you to face various emergencies, whether in the wilderness or urban environments. This book is designed to be your comprehensive guide, offering practical and actionable advice to develop these skills. As you journey through its pages, you will encounter information that could one day save your life or the lives of others. Understanding how to use this book effectively will enhance your learning experience and ensure you can apply the skills in real-world scenarios.

Begin by familiarizing yourself with the overall structure of the book. The content is thoughtfully organized into distinct sections, each covering crucial aspects of survival. The chapters flow logically, starting with foundational concepts and progressing to more advanced techniques. This arrangement allows you to build your knowledge systematically. Whether you are a beginner or someone with some survival experience, following the chapters in sequence will help you develop a holistic understanding of survival skills.

Each chapter starts with a brief introduction to the topic, setting the stage for the detailed information that follows. These introductions are meant to provide context and highlight the importance of the skills you are about to learn. Pay close attention to these sections as they often include insights into why certain skills are vital and how they can be applied in various situations. This context will help you appreciate the relevance of the information and stay motivated to absorb the details.

While reading, take notes and highlight key points. This active engagement with the material will reinforce your learning and make it easier to review important concepts later. Consider keeping a dedicated notebook or digital document where you can jot down critical information, personal reflections, and any questions that arise. Revisiting these notes periodically will solidify your understanding and keep the knowledge fresh in your mind.

Practical application is a cornerstone of learning survival skills. As you read through each chapter, look for opportunities to practice what you have learned. For instance, when you reach the section on fire-starting techniques, gather the necessary materials and attempt to start a fire using the methods described. Hands-on practice not only reinforces theoretical knowledge but also builds muscle memory, making you more proficient in executing the skills under pressure.

Survival scenarios often require quick thinking and adaptability. To prepare for this, engage in regular drills and simulations. Create hypothetical situations based on the scenarios described in the book and practice your response. For example, simulate a situation where you need to find and purify water in the wilderness or navigate through an urban disaster. These exercises will help you develop the ability to think on your feet and apply your skills effectively in real emergencies.

The book also emphasizes mental resilience and situational awareness, critical components of survival. As you read about these topics, reflect on your current mental state and awareness levels. Consider incorporating mindfulness practices into your daily routine to enhance your mental resilience. Simple exercises like deep breathing, meditation, and visualization can improve your ability to stay calm and focused in high-stress situations. Developing situational awareness involves being more observant of your surroundings and understanding potential threats and resources. Practice this by taking note of exits, landmarks, and environmental cues in your daily life.

Another effective way to use this book is to form a study group or join a survival skills community. Learning alongside others provides a support system and allows you to exchange knowledge and experiences. Discussing the material with peers can offer new perspectives and insights that you might not have considered. Additionally, practicing skills in a group setting can simulate real-world scenarios where teamwork and communication are essential.

Throughout the book, you will encounter various tips, tricks, and anecdotes that enrich your understanding of survival skills. These elements are designed to make the material more engaging and relatable. Take the time to read these sections carefully, as they often contain valuable lessons learned from real-life experiences. Stories of survival can be particularly inspiring and serve as powerful reminders of the importance of the skills you are developing.

The book also includes detailed illustrations and diagrams to complement the written instructions. Visual aids can be incredibly helpful in understanding complex techniques or processes. When you come across these visuals, study them closely and compare them to the written descriptions. This dual approach can enhance your comprehension and ensure you can replicate the techniques accurately.

To maximize the benefits of this book, set specific goals for your learning. Identify the skills you want to master and create a timeline for achieving them. Breaking down your learning into manageable tasks can prevent overwhelm and keep you motivated. For example, you might set a goal to learn and practice three new fire-starting techniques within a month or to complete a full wilderness survival simulation by the end of the season. Tracking your progress and celebrating milestones will make the learning process more enjoyable and rewarding.

In addition to the core content, the book offers resources for further learning. These may include recommended readings, websites, and instructional videos. Utilize these resources to deepen your knowledge and explore topics in greater detail. Continuous learning is essential in the field of survival skills, as new techniques and information are constantly emerging. Staying informed and updating your skills regularly will ensure you are always prepared for any situation.

As you progress through the book, remember that survival skills are not just about individual capabilities but also about helping others. The knowledge you gain can be invaluable in assisting friends, family, or even strangers in emergencies. Consider sharing what you learn with those around you and encouraging them to develop their own survival skills. Building a community of prepared individuals can create a network of support that enhances everyone's safety and resilience.

Finally, treat this book as a living document. Your understanding and proficiency in survival skills will evolve over time, and so should your approach to using this book. Revisit chapters periodically to refresh your knowledge and update your techniques. Reflect on your experiences and how they align with the information presented. This iterative process will ensure that your survival skills remain sharp and relevant.

By using this book effectively, you are taking a proactive step towards ensuring your safety and preparedness in any situation. Embrace the journey of learning and practicing survival skills, knowing that the effort you invest today can make a significant difference when faced with unforeseen challenges. Stay committed, stay curious, and most importantly, stay prepared.

Survival skills serve as a critical bridge between human vulnerability and resilience, especially when faced with unexpected challenges in both wilderness and urban environments. Understanding the fundamental differences and similarities between these two types of survival can prepare you for a wide range of scenarios, each requiring unique strategies and mindsets.

In the wilderness, survival hinges on your ability to adapt to a natural environment that can be both beautiful and brutal. Imagine finding yourself amidst dense forests, arid deserts, or mountainous terrains without the comforts and conveniences of modern life. The key to wilderness survival lies in mastering the basics: sourcing water, building shelter, making fire, and finding food. These skills are not just about knowledge but also about practice and the ability to remain calm under pressure.

Water is the cornerstone of survival in any environment. In the wilderness, it's crucial to locate a natural water source, such as a river, stream, or lake. However, even clear-looking water can harbor harmful pathogens. Techniques such as boiling water, using portable filtration systems, or applying purification tablets can make water safe to drink. Collecting rainwater using tarps or other materials can also be an effective method. Always prioritize water purification to prevent dehydration and waterborne diseases.

Building a shelter is another fundamental skill in wilderness survival. Protection from the elements—whether it's scorching sun, freezing temperatures, or torrential rain—is vital. A good shelter conserves body heat and shields you from the weather. You might construct a lean-to using branches and foliage, or create a debris hut insulated with leaves and grass. In snowy conditions, a snow cave can provide warmth. The materials and techniques will vary based on your environment, but the principles of insulation and wind protection remain constant.

Fire serves multiple purposes in a survival situation: warmth, protection, cooking, and signaling for help. Starting a fire in the wilderness often requires more than just a lighter or matches; understanding alternative methods, such as using flint and steel, a bow drill, or a fire plow, can be lifesaving. Gathering dry tinder, kindling, and fuel wood is essential, and practicing fire-making skills in various conditions (wet, windy, cold) will enhance your proficiency.

Food is less immediate a concern than water or shelter but still crucial for long-term survival. Foraging for edible plants, berries, and nuts requires knowledge of local flora to avoid poisonous species. Basic trapping and fishing skills can supplement your diet with protein. Learning to set snares, build fish traps, and identify animal tracks can provide essential nutrition. Insects, while less appetizing, are a viable food source rich in protein and should not be overlooked in a survival scenario.

Mental resilience and situational awareness are equally important in the wilderness. Staying calm and focused can prevent panic, which often leads to poor decision-making. Regularly assessing your surroundings and resources, understanding weather patterns, and anticipating potential threats (like predators or hazardous terrain) will help you make informed decisions.

Transitioning to urban survival, the challenges and strategies shift significantly. Urban environments, while familiar, can become hostile quickly during disasters such as earthquakes, hurricanes, or civil unrest. Here, survival often depends on navigating structural hazards, finding safe shelter, and dealing with potential scarcity of resources.

In urban settings, water sources might include public fountains, water heaters, or even toilet tanks (not bowls). Purification remains crucial, as municipal systems can become contaminated. Having portable filters, purification tablets, or knowledge of basic distillation techniques can ensure a safe supply of water.

Finding shelter in an urban environment may involve identifying structurally sound buildings, avoiding areas with potential collapse risks, and securing entry points. Knowing how to barricade doors, create makeshift beds, and find warmth without electricity are valuable skills. Urban shelters should also provide concealment and security from potential threats, including other people.

Fire-making in urban settings might be less about warmth and more about cooking, boiling water, or signaling. Understanding how to safely use available resources—like gas stoves, fireplaces, or portable stoves—is crucial. In the absence of traditional fire-making materials, improvisation skills come into play. Always be mindful of ventilation to avoid carbon monoxide poisoning.

Food procurement in a city involves a mix of scavenging, foraging, and rationing. Identifying viable food sources, such as canned goods, dried foods, and even edible plants growing in parks or abandoned lots, can sustain you. Knowing how to safely access and prepare these foods, while avoiding spoilage and contamination, is essential. In prolonged situations, bartering and community cooperation can become vital for food security.

Safety and first aid are paramount in both environments, but urban settings may present unique medical challenges, such as injuries from debris or conflicts. Basic first aid knowledge, including wound care, CPR, and recognizing signs of infections, can save lives. Having a well-stocked first aid kit and knowing how to improvise medical supplies from available resources can be lifesaving.

Communication and information access are critical in urban survival. Understanding how to use radios, staying informed through emergency broadcasts, and having a plan for reconnecting with loved ones can provide a significant advantage. In the absence of electronic communication, traditional methods like signal fires, mirrors, or written messages can still be effective.

Ultimately, the mindset for survival in both wilderness and urban settings involves adaptability, resourcefulness, and resilience. Each environment presents its own set of challenges and requires tailored strategies. However, the core principles—securing water, shelter, fire, and food, while maintaining mental and physical health—remain universal.

In both scenarios, continuous learning and practice are essential. Regularly updating your knowledge, practicing skills in controlled conditions, and staying physically fit will prepare you for unexpected situations. Building a community of like-minded individuals can also provide mutual support and increase your chances of survival.

Embrace the journey of learning these survival skills, understanding that they empower you to face uncertainties with confidence. By mastering the fundamentals of both wilderness and urban survival, you equip yourself with the tools to navigate and overcome the challenges posed by any environment. Whether you find yourself lost in the wild or navigating a post-disaster city, your preparedness and resilience will be your greatest assets.

When it comes to survival, clear and well-defined goals are not just beneficial; they are essential. Setting survival goals provides direction and purpose, which are crucial when facing the unpredictable challenges that nature or urban environments can throw at you. Without goals, it is easy to become overwhelmed and unfocused, leading to poor decision-making and decreased chances of survival. Establishing survival goals requires a blend of foresight, practical knowledge, and adaptability.

Imagine you are suddenly thrust into a survival situation. The initial shock can be paralyzing, but having pre-set goals can help you prioritize your actions and remain calm. The first step in setting survival goals is to assess your immediate needs and resources. This involves a quick but thorough evaluation of your physical condition, the environment, available supplies, and potential threats. Your primary goal should always be to ensure your immediate safety, which includes finding or creating shelter, securing a water source, and building a fire if necessary.

Shelter is often your first line of defense against the elements. Whether you are in a dense forest, a barren desert, or a concrete jungle, protecting yourself from harsh weather conditions is paramount. In a cold environment, your goal might be to construct an insulated shelter that conserves body heat. In a hot climate, finding shade and ventilation becomes critical. The materials and methods for building a shelter will vary, but the underlying goal remains the same: to create a safe space where you can rest and recover.

Securing a reliable water source is another immediate goal. Humans can survive for weeks without food but only a few days without water. Identifying sources of water, such as streams, rivers, or even dew, is a priority. Once located, the water must be purified to ensure it is safe to drink. This can involve boiling, filtering, or using chemical purification tablets. Your goal should be to establish a routine for collecting and purifying water to maintain hydration consistently.

Fire serves multiple purposes in survival situations, from providing warmth and a means to cook food to serving as a signal for rescuers. Your goal should be to learn various fire-starting techniques that do not rely solely on modern conveniences like lighters or matches. Skills such as using a bow drill, flint and steel, or even a magnifying glass can be invaluable. Practice these methods regularly to ensure you can create fire even under challenging conditions.

Food procurement is a longer-term survival goal but still critical. Depending on your environment, this may involve foraging for edible plants, hunting, fishing, or trapping. Familiarize yourself with the local flora and fauna, and learn to identify safe and nutritious food sources. Setting traps, fishing lines, or creating small game snares can provide a steady supply of protein. Your goal should be to develop a sustainable method of food acquisition that does not deplete the local resources too quickly.

Mental resilience is a crucial, often underestimated, survival goal. The psychological strain of a survival situation can be as debilitating as physical threats. Setting goals to maintain a positive mindset, manage stress, and stay motivated can make a significant difference. Techniques such as mindfulness, visualization, and setting small, achievable daily tasks can help maintain morale. Remember, the will to survive is a powerful tool.

In an urban survival scenario, your goals might shift slightly to accommodate the different challenges posed by a built environment. Safety from structural hazards, finding secure shelter, and dealing with potential human threats become priorities. Your goal should be to quickly identify safe zones, such as structurally sound buildings or designated emergency shelters. Urban environments might offer more immediate resources like food and water, but accessing them safely can be a challenge. Establishing a secure base of operations from which you can plan and execute your survival strategies is crucial.

Communication and information become vital goals in urban survival. Knowing how to stay informed about the evolving situation, whether through radios, mobile devices, or community networks, can provide critical advantages. Your goal should be to establish reliable means of communication to stay connected with potential rescuers or to gather information about safe zones and resources.

In both wilderness and urban settings, long-term survival goals should include plans for self-rescue or signaling for help. Understanding basic navigation skills, such as using a compass, reading maps, or even navigating by the stars, can guide you to safety. Similarly, knowing how to signal for help using fire, mirrors, or signal flares increases your chances of being found by rescuers. Your goal should be to continuously improve these skills and have a plan for self-rescue if waiting for external help is not viable.

Health and hygiene are often overlooked but critical survival goals. Preventing illness and injury can significantly increase your chances of survival. Your goals should include maintaining cleanliness to avoid infections, managing waste, and knowing basic first aid. Carrying a well-stocked first aid kit and learning how to use its contents effectively can be lifesaving. Regularly check and update your first aid knowledge and supplies to ensure they are ready when needed.

Finally, adaptability is the underlying goal that ties all others together. Survival situations are dynamic and can change rapidly. Being able to reassess your goals, adapt to new information, and remain flexible in your approach is crucial. This might mean altering your shelter plans due to unexpected weather changes, finding new water sources if the original one is compromised, or adjusting your food procurement methods as local resources fluctuate. Embrace a mindset of continuous learning and adaptability.

Setting survival goals is not a one-time task but an ongoing process. Review and adjust your goals regularly, both in practice scenarios and real-life situations. This continuous assessment ensures that your goals remain relevant and achievable as circumstances evolve. By setting clear, actionable goals and remaining adaptable, you can navigate the complexities of any survival situation with confidence and resilience.

Imagine waking up one day to find yourself thrust into an unexpected survival scenario. Whether it's a natural disaster, a sudden loss of resources, or an isolated wilderness situation, the mental fortitude you bring to the table can make all the difference. Preparing mentally for survival scenarios is as crucial as learning practical skills like building a fire or finding water. Your mind is your most powerful tool, capable of navigating the complexities and stresses of survival situations.

The first step in mental preparation is understanding the nature of survival psychology. When faced with life-threatening situations, our brains instinctively react with a "fight or flight" response. This primal reaction can be beneficial, providing a burst of energy and heightened awareness. However, it can also lead to panic, clouded judgment, and poor decision-making. Recognizing this response and learning to control it is vital.

Developing a resilient mindset is essential. Resilience, in the context of survival, means the ability to recover quickly from difficulties and adapt to changing circumstances. One way to build resilience is through stress inoculation training. This involves exposing yourself to controlled, manageable stressors to build your tolerance and coping mechanisms. For example, practicing survival skills in a safe, controlled environment can help you become more comfortable with the pressures you'll face in a real situation.

Visualization is another powerful tool. Athletes and performers often use visualization to prepare for high-stress events, and the same technique can be applied to survival scenarios. Spend time imagining yourself in various survival situations. Visualize the steps you would take, the challenges you'd face, and how you would overcome them. This mental rehearsal can help reduce anxiety and increase confidence when you find yourself in an actual survival situation.

Maintaining a positive attitude is crucial for survival. Optimism can be a powerful motivator, helping you to persevere through difficult times. However, it's important to balance optimism with realism. Acknowledge the seriousness of your situation, but focus on what you can control and the steps you can take to improve your circumstances. Setting small, achievable goals is a great way to maintain a positive outlook. Each small victory, whether it's finding water or starting a fire, can boost your morale and keep you motivated.

Self-awareness plays a key role in mental preparation. Understanding your strengths and weaknesses allows you to better prepare for survival scenarios. Take stock of your physical and mental capabilities. Are you physically fit enough to endure long hikes or strenuous activities? How do you typically respond to stress? Knowing the answers to these questions can help you develop a more effective survival plan.

Another critical aspect of mental preparation is the ability to stay calm under pressure. Panic is one of the biggest enemies in a survival situation. It can lead to rash decisions and wasted energy. Practice techniques for staying calm, such as deep breathing, mindfulness, and grounding exercises. These techniques can help you keep a clear head and make rational decisions, even in the face of danger.

Flexibility and adaptability are also paramount. Survival situations are unpredictable and constantly changing. The ability to adapt your plans and strategies to new information and circumstances can greatly increase your chances of survival. This might mean changing your route when faced with an unexpected obstacle or finding alternative food sources when your initial plan fails. Embrace a mindset of continuous learning and adaptability.

Building a survival mentality also involves preparing for the potential emotional toll. Loneliness, fear, and despair are common emotions in survival scenarios. Acknowledge these feelings and develop strategies to cope with them. For example, maintaining a routine, even a simple one, can provide a sense of normalcy and control. Engaging in small, enjoyable activities, like reading a book or journaling, can help keep your spirits up.

One often overlooked aspect of mental preparation is the importance of social connections. Humans are inherently social creatures, and having a support network can be a tremendous asset in a survival situation. Whether it's family, friends, or a survival group, knowing that you have people who care about you and are willing to help can provide a significant psychological boost. If you find yourself alone, creating a sense of companionship, even with a pet or through imaginary conversations, can help combat loneliness and maintain mental health.

Training and practice are vital components of mental preparation. Just as you would practice building a shelter or purifying water, you should also practice mental skills. Conduct regular drills and simulations to test your mental preparedness. These exercises can help you identify areas for improvement and build confidence in your ability to handle real-world situations.

Finally, never underestimate the power of knowledge. Educate yourself about survival psychology, stress management, and mental resilience. Read books, take courses, and learn from experts. The more you know, the better equipped you'll be to handle the mental challenges of a survival scenario.

In conclusion, preparing mentally for survival scenarios is a multifaceted process that involves building resilience, practicing stress management techniques, maintaining a positive attitude, and continuously learning and adapting. By focusing on these aspects, you can enhance your mental preparedness and increase your chances of surviving and thriving in even the most challenging situations.

Chapter 2 : The Survival Mindset

Building Mental Resilience

Surviving in the wild or during a crisis demands more than just physical preparedness; it requires a sturdy mental foundation. Building mental resilience is about developing the inner strength to cope with stress, adversity, and uncertainty. This resilience doesn't come overnight, but through a series of deliberate practices and mindset shifts that prepare you to face and overcome challenges.

Consider the story of Tom, an avid hiker who found himself lost in the dense wilderness after a wrong turn. With no immediate way out, his mental resilience was put to the test. Despite the initial panic, Tom relied on his mental training to stay calm, focus on immediate tasks, and maintain hope. He survived for days on minimal rations and eventually found his way back to safety. His story underscores the importance of mental resilience in survival situations.

A critical aspect of building mental resilience is developing a positive mindset. This doesn't mean ignoring the severity of the situation, but rather focusing on what you can control and finding silver linings. Optimism can fuel the will to survive and inspire creative problem-solving. For example, rather than dwelling on the scarcity of food, focus on the skills you have to find or hunt for more. Remember, a positive attitude can be as nourishing as food itself in dire circumstances.

However, positivity must be tempered with realism. It's essential to set achievable goals and acknowledge the difficulties you face. Unrealistic optimism can lead to disappointment and demoralization. Balance is key—maintain hope, but ground it in reality. This combination can provide the motivation to keep going while preparing you for setbacks.

Self-awareness is another cornerstone of mental resilience. Understanding your strengths and weaknesses allows you to leverage your capabilities and seek help or develop skills where needed. Regular self-reflection can enhance this awareness. Consider keeping a journal where you record your thoughts, feelings, and behaviors. Over time, this practice can reveal patterns and help you understand how you cope with stress, enabling you to refine your strategies.

Stress management techniques are vital for maintaining mental resilience. The body's natural response to stress—the fight or flight mechanism—can be both a boon and a bane. While it can heighten your senses and provide a burst of energy, prolonged stress can lead to fatigue and impaired judgment. Learning to manage stress through techniques like deep breathing, meditation, and progressive muscle relaxation can keep you calm and focused.

Deep breathing, for instance, can be practiced anywhere and at any time. When you feel overwhelmed, take a moment to inhale deeply through your nose, hold for a few seconds, and exhale slowly through your mouth. This simple exercise can slow your heart rate and clear your mind, making it easier to think logically and make sound decisions.

Building mental resilience also involves cultivating a sense of purpose. Having a clear reason to survive—whether it's to reunite with loved ones, fulfill a personal mission, or simply the will to live—can provide the drive needed to push through hardships. Reflect on your motivations and keep them at the forefront of your mind during challenging times. This sense of purpose acts as a north star, guiding you through the darkest moments.

Social connections are another powerful factor in building mental resilience. Humans are inherently social beings, and having a support network can significantly bolster your mental strength. Even in isolation, maintaining a sense of connection through memories, letters, or imagined conversations can provide comfort and reduce feelings of loneliness. If you're with others, fostering a sense of camaraderie and mutual support can enhance the group's overall resilience.

Adaptability is a key trait of resilient individuals. Survival situations are unpredictable, and rigid plans can quickly become obsolete. Being able to adapt your strategies and remain flexible in your approach is crucial. Embrace change and view challenges as opportunities to learn and grow. This mindset can turn obstacles into stepping stones and reduce the mental strain of constantly shifting circumstances.

Physical health and mental resilience are deeply interconnected. Regular exercise, adequate sleep, and a balanced diet can enhance your mental strength. Exercise, in particular, releases endorphins that elevate mood and reduce stress. In a survival situation, maintaining physical health might be challenging, but even simple activities like stretching or light exercises can help keep your body and mind in better shape.

Another component of mental resilience is the ability to manage emotions effectively. It's natural to experience fear, anger, and sadness in survival situations. However, allowing these emotions to overwhelm you can be detrimental. Practice acknowledging your emotions without letting them control your actions. Techniques such as mindfulness and cognitive behavioral strategies can help you process emotions constructively.

Mindfulness involves staying present and fully engaging with the current moment, rather than getting lost in fears about the future or regrets about the past. This practice can be as simple as paying attention to your surroundings, the sensations in your body, or your breathing. By grounding yourself in the present, you can reduce anxiety and improve your focus.

Cognitive behavioral strategies involve identifying and challenging negative thought patterns. For example, if you find yourself thinking, "I can't do this," counter that thought with evidence of your past successes and strengths. Replacing negative thoughts with positive, realistic ones can change your perspective and boost your resilience.

Finally, continuous learning and skill development are essential for building mental resilience. The more skills and knowledge you have, the more confident and capable you'll feel in survival situations. Take every opportunity to learn new survival techniques, whether it's through formal training, reading, or hands-on practice. This proactive approach not only prepares you for practical challenges but also strengthens your mental resilience by fostering a growth mindset.

In summary, building mental resilience is a multifaceted process involving a positive yet realistic mindset, self-awareness, stress management, a sense of purpose, social connections, adaptability, physical health, emotional regulation, and continuous learning. By cultivating these qualities, you can enhance your ability to face and overcome the challenges of survival situations, emerging stronger and more resilient.

The ability to stay calm and focused under pressure is a cornerstone of survival. When faced with a crisis, whether it's a sudden natural disaster, a life-threatening situation, or an unexpected wilderness challenge, maintaining composure can be the difference between life and death. Your mind, when clear and focused, can help you think critically, make better decisions, and utilize your resources effectively.

Picture a scenario where you're stranded in the mountains after a hiking trip goes awry. The weather is turning, night is falling, and you realize you're lost. Panic is a natural initial reaction, but it's crucial to manage it quickly. Panic clouds judgment and can lead to poor decisions. Instead, a calm and focused mind will allow you to assess your situation, prioritize your actions, and execute a plan efficiently.

One of the most effective techniques to stay calm is controlled breathing. When you feel panic rising, take a moment to focus on your breath. Inhale deeply through your nose for a count of four, hold for four, and exhale through your mouth for four. This simple practice, often referred to as box breathing, can slow your heart rate and bring clarity to your mind. Regular practice of this technique can make it second nature in high-stress situations.

Another method to maintain focus is grounding yourself in the present moment. In a crisis, your mind might race with worries about the future or regrets about past decisions. Grounding techniques, such as focusing on the physical sensations around you—like the feel of the ground under your feet, the sound of the wind, or the smell of the forest—can bring your attention back to the present. This mindfulness practice helps prevent your mind from spiraling and keeps you centered on what you need to do right now.

Setting clear, achievable goals is another strategy to maintain focus. When faced with a daunting situation, break it down into manageable tasks. For example, if you're lost in the wilderness, your immediate goals might be finding shelter, securing water, and signaling for help. By focusing on these smaller, tangible objectives, you can prevent yourself from becoming overwhelmed by the gravity of the overall situation. Each small success builds confidence and keeps you moving forward.

Visualization can also be a powerful tool. Elite athletes often use visualization to prepare for competitions, and you can use it to prepare for survival scenarios. Close your eyes and imagine yourself successfully navigating the challenge at hand. Picture each step clearly, from starting a fire to finding your way back to safety. This mental rehearsal can increase your confidence and prepare your mind and body for the real thing.

Maintaining a positive internal dialogue is critical. The way you talk to yourself can significantly impact your stress levels and ability to stay focused. Replace negative thoughts with positive affirmations. Instead of thinking, "I can't handle this," tell yourself, "I am capable and prepared." These affirmations remind you of your skills and strengths, bolstering your confidence and ability to stay calm.

Another aspect to consider is the importance of preparation. The more prepared you are, the less likely you are to panic when things go wrong. This preparation includes not only physical skills and supplies but also mental readiness. Regularly practicing survival skills, participating in simulations, and studying survival techniques can build a reservoir of knowledge and confidence that you can draw on in a crisis.

Mental and physical health are deeply intertwined. Regular physical exercise, a healthy diet, and adequate sleep can improve your overall resilience to stress. Exercise, in particular, releases endorphins, which can enhance your mood and reduce anxiety. A fit body also means a more efficient response to physical challenges, which can further reduce stress.

Social support is another critical factor. If you're with others during a crisis, maintaining open communication and supporting each other can help everyone stay calm. Share your feelings, listen to others, and work together to solve problems. This sense of camaraderie can provide emotional strength and distribute the burden of decision-making, reducing individual stress.

Adaptability is also crucial in maintaining calm and focus. Survival situations are often fluid, with circumstances changing rapidly. Being able to adapt your plans and remain flexible in your approach can help you stay calm. Rigid thinking can lead to frustration and panic when things don't go as expected. Embrace the mindset that change is inevitable and be prepared to adjust your strategies as needed.

Knowledge and continuous learning are vital. The more you know about survival techniques, the less likely you are to panic when faced with a challenge. Educate yourself on various survival scenarios, learn from experts, and practice regularly. This ongoing learning process builds confidence and reduces the fear of the unknown.

Managing emotions effectively is another key component. It's natural to feel fear, anger, or sadness in a survival situation, but these emotions can cloud your judgment. Acknowledge your emotions without letting them control your actions. Techniques such as journaling, talking to a trusted companion, or even a simple scream into the wilderness can help release pent-up emotions constructively.

Lastly, spiritual practices or personal rituals can provide comfort and focus in times of crisis. Whether it's prayer, meditation, or simply repeating a mantra, these practices can offer a sense of peace and stability. They remind you of your inner strength and the larger picture, providing solace and direction.

In essence, staying calm and focused in a survival situation is a multifaceted skill that involves controlled breathing, mindfulness, goal setting, positive self-talk, preparation, physical fitness, social support, adaptability, continuous learning, emotional management, and spiritual practices. By cultivating these habits and skills, you can prepare your mind to handle the stress and uncertainty of survival scenarios, ultimately enhancing your chances of making it through safely.

Imagine you're hiking through a dense forest, the canopy above turning the late afternoon light into a mosaic of green shadows. You're enjoying the tranquility when suddenly, you hear a rustling sound nearby. It could be the wind, or it could be an animal. Your heart rate quickens, and your senses heighten. This moment calls for acute situational awareness—a skill that could save your life in the wild or during any crisis.

Situational awareness is the ability to perceive, understand, and react to your environment. It's about knowing what's happening around you and anticipating what could happen next. In survival scenarios, this skill is crucial. It enables you to detect threats early, make informed decisions, and take appropriate actions swiftly.

The foundation of situational awareness is observation. This begins with consciously taking in your surroundings. Use all your senses—sight, sound, smell, touch, and even taste when appropriate. Look around and note the terrain, weather conditions, and any wildlife. Listen for unusual sounds, like the snap of a twig or the distant roar of water. Smell the air for smoke, which could indicate a fire, or the scent of water sources. Feel the ground beneath your feet; different textures can signal changes in terrain. This sensory input forms the basis of your situational awareness.

Consider the story of Sarah, an experienced hiker. While trekking through a remote mountain range, she noticed subtle changes in the environment: birds suddenly stopped singing, and the air felt heavier. These observations made her pause and look more closely. She then spotted fresh bear tracks on the trail. Thanks to her heightened awareness, she was able to take a detour and avoid a potentially dangerous encounter with a bear. Sarah's story illustrates the importance of keen observation and how it can lead to safer decisions.

Once you've gathered sensory information, the next step is to interpret it. This involves understanding what the data means and how it relates to your situation. For instance, if you hear running water, it could indicate a nearby stream, which is essential for hydration. However, it could also mean you're near a waterfall or rapids, which could be dangerous if you need to cross. Interpretation requires knowledge and experience. The more you know about your environment and the potential hazards, the better you can make sense of what you observe.

Memory plays a significant role in interpretation. Remembering previous experiences and the outcomes of past decisions can guide you in the present. For example, if you've encountered a similar rustling sound in the forest before and it turned out to be a harmless deer, you might feel less alarmed. However, if it was a predator last time, you'd know to proceed with caution. Keeping a mental or written log of your observations and experiences can enhance your situational awareness over time.

Anticipation is the next critical element. Based on your observations and interpretations, you should be able to predict potential developments. This means thinking ahead and considering various scenarios. What if the weather suddenly changes? What if you encounter a wild animal? What if you get injured? Anticipating these possibilities allows you to prepare mentally and physically, enhancing your readiness to respond.

Let's revisit Sarah's situation. After noticing the bear tracks, she didn't just change her route and forget about it. She anticipated that the bear might still be in the area. She kept her senses alert, moved cautiously, and ensured she had her bear spray within easy reach. Her ability to anticipate further potential encounters with the bear kept her vigilant and ready to act if necessary.

Effective situational awareness also involves managing your mental state. Stress, fatigue, and emotions like fear or excitement can cloud your judgment and reduce your awareness. It's essential to stay calm and composed, even in high-pressure situations. Techniques such as deep breathing, mindfulness, and mental rehearsals can help maintain a clear mind. Regular breaks to rest and hydrate can also keep your mind sharp and your senses keen.

Another aspect of situational awareness is understanding human behavior, both your own and others'. Knowing how people, including yourself, might react in different situations can inform your decisions and actions. For example, in a group, some individuals might panic under stress, while others might freeze. Recognizing these tendencies can help you manage group dynamics and ensure everyone's safety.

Communication is crucial when you're with others. Share your observations and interpretations with your group. Discuss potential scenarios and agree on a plan of action. This collective awareness can enhance safety and efficiency. In Sarah's case, if she had been with a group, she would have needed to communicate her findings about the bear tracks and coordinate the detour to keep everyone safe.

Situational awareness also involves continuous learning and adaptation. The environment can change rapidly, and new information can emerge at any moment. Stay flexible and be ready to update your understanding and plans accordingly. This might mean taking a new route, changing your pace, or finding a new shelter. The more adaptable you are, the better you can respond to changing circumstances.

Training and practice are essential for developing and refining situational awareness. Regularly put yourself in scenarios where you need to observe, interpret, and anticipate. This could be through outdoor activities like hiking, camping, orienteering, or even urban exploration. Simulated survival scenarios and drills can also be valuable. The more you practice, the more intuitive situational awareness becomes.

Technology can aid situational awareness, but it should not be relied upon entirely. Tools like GPS, weather apps, and communication devices can provide valuable information, but they can also fail or give a false sense of security. Always complement technological tools with your observations and judgment. For instance, a GPS might show a clear path, but your senses might detect a recent landslide that blocks the way. Trust your instincts and use technology as a supplementary aid.

Personal health and fitness contribute to situational awareness. A healthy, well-nourished body supports a sharp mind. Regular physical exercise, a balanced diet, and sufficient rest can enhance your sensory perceptions and cognitive functions. In a survival situation, your physical condition can directly impact your ability to observe, interpret, and respond effectively.

In summary, developing situational awareness is a multifaceted process that involves keen observation, accurate interpretation, anticipation of potential scenarios, and continuous adaptation. It requires a calm and composed mind, effective communication, and regular practice. By honing these skills, you can significantly enhance your ability to navigate and survive in challenging environments, ensuring safety and success in the face of adversity.

The moment you find yourself in a high-stress situation, your ability to make clear, decisive choices can spell the difference between success and failure, safety and danger, life and death. Whether you're lost in a forest, facing an unexpected storm, or dealing with an injured companion, decision-making under pressure is a skill that can be developed and honed. This chapter will delve into practical strategies and real-world examples to help you make sound decisions when the stakes are high.

One of the primary barriers to effective decision-making in high-stress situations is the overwhelming sense of urgency and panic that can cloud your judgment. When your heart races and your mind spirals into worst-case scenarios, it's crucial to regain control over your emotions. Controlled breathing is a simple yet powerful technique to calm your nerves and clear your mind. Inhale deeply through your nose for a count of four, hold for four, and exhale through your mouth for four. This method, often referred to as box breathing, can help slow your heart rate and bring clarity to your thoughts.

Imagine being caught in a sudden snowstorm during a mountain hike. Visibility drops to near zero, and the temperature plummets. Panic can set in quickly, leading to hasty and often poor decisions. By practicing controlled breathing, you can create a moment of calm amidst the chaos, allowing you to think more clearly. This pause gives you the opportunity to evaluate your situation logically rather than reacting impulsively.

Once you've calmed your immediate physiological response, it's time to assess your situation systematically. Start by gathering all available information. What do you see, hear, and feel? Are there immediate threats you need to address, such as an unstable environment or a physical injury? Understanding your environment and the resources at your disposal is the first step in making an informed decision.

Consider the story of John, an experienced sailor who found himself adrift in a severe storm. His boat was taking on water, and the radio was dead. Instead of letting fear take over, John took a moment to breathe deeply and assess his situation. He checked the integrity of his boat, identified the most significant leaks, and used available materials to slow the flooding. By methodically addressing each problem, John kept his boat afloat until the storm passed, demonstrating the importance of a structured approach to decision-making.

Prioritizing tasks is essential once you have a clear understanding of your situation. In high-stress scenarios, there are often multiple issues competing for your attention. Use the prioritization method known as the "ABCDE" framework—Airway, Breathing, Circulation, Disability, Exposure. This model is particularly useful in medical emergencies but can be adapted to other situations by focusing first on the most critical threats to life and health.

For instance, if you're lost in the wilderness and nightfall is approaching, your priorities might be securing shelter, finding a water source, and signaling for help. Establishing a clear order of tasks helps prevent the paralysis that can occur when faced with too many simultaneous demands.

Decision-making also benefits greatly from having established protocols and plans. When you've practiced and internalized certain procedures, they become second nature, reducing the cognitive load during a crisis. This is why pilots, astronauts, and emergency responders train rigorously on specific protocols—they don't have to invent solutions under pressure; they follow a practiced script.

Take the example of Susan, a nurse who encountered a multi-car accident on her way home. Despite the chaos, she immediately reverted to her training: she assessed the scene for safety, called emergency services, and began triaging the injured. Her ability to fall back on established protocols allowed her to act swiftly and effectively, providing critical care until help arrived.

In addition to protocols, developing mental models can aid in quick decision-making. Mental models are frameworks that help simplify complex situations. For instance, the OODA Loop—Observe, Orient, Decide, Act—is a model used by the military to make rapid decisions in dynamic environments. By continuously cycling through these four stages, you can stay adaptive and responsive to changing conditions.

Imagine you're kayaking in a river when you suddenly encounter a series of unexpected rapids. Using the OODA Loop, you first observe the immediate environment, noting the speed and direction of the water. Next, you orient yourself by considering your position relative to the obstacles. You then decide on the best path forward and act by paddling decisively. This iterative process helps maintain flexibility and responsiveness, critical in high-stress situations.

Another critical aspect of decision-making under pressure is managing cognitive biases. Stress can exacerbate biases, leading you to make poor choices based on incomplete or skewed information. Common biases include the confirmation bias, where you favor information that confirms your preconceptions, and the availability heuristic, where you rely on immediate examples that come to mind.

To counteract these biases, make a conscious effort to seek out diverse perspectives and challenge your assumptions. If you're in a group, encourage open discussion and listen to others' viewpoints. This can help surface critical information you might have overlooked and provide a more balanced view of the situation.

Consider the case of a rescue team responding to a natural disaster. The team leader, aware of the confirmation bias, actively seeks input from all team members before making decisions. By valuing diverse perspectives, the leader ensures that no critical detail is missed, leading to more effective and comprehensive action plans.

Maintaining adaptability is another key element of effective decision-making. High-stress situations are often fluid, with conditions changing rapidly. The plan that seems perfect one moment might become untenable the next. Being rigid in your approach can lead to failure, whereas flexibility allows you to pivot and adjust as needed.

Think about an expedition team on a glacier climb. When an unexpected crevasse blocks their planned route, the leader doesn't insist on sticking to the original path. Instead, they quickly assess alternative routes, weigh the risks, and decide on a new course. This adaptability ensures the team's safety and progress, illustrating the importance of being willing to change plans based on new information.

Lastly, reflection after the fact is crucial for improving future decision-making. After the high-stress event has passed, take the time to debrief and analyze what happened. What decisions were made, and why? What worked well, and what could have been done differently? Learning from each experience builds a repository of knowledge that enhances your ability to handle future crises.

In summary, decision-making in high-stress situations requires a combination of emotional control, systematic assessment, prioritization, established protocols, mental models, bias management, adaptability, and post-event reflection. By developing these skills and approaches, you can improve your ability to make sound, effective decisions when it matters most.

Survival situations often test the human spirit in unprecedented ways. Faced with extreme environments, limited resources, and potential isolation, the will to survive becomes a critical element in overcoming these challenges. This chapter delves into the psychological and emotional aspects of survival, demonstrating how a strong will can make a difference between life and death.

Imagine being stranded in the wilderness after a plane crash. The initial shock is overwhelming. Your body aches, and the wreckage around you is a stark reminder of the fragility of life. In such moments, the human mind can either become your greatest ally or your worst enemy. The will to survive is not just about physical endurance; it's about mental resilience and the ability to harness inner strength.

One of the first steps in cultivating the will to survive is to manage fear. Fear is a natural response to danger, but it can be paralyzing. When confronted with a life-threatening situation, it's essential to acknowledge your fear without letting it control you. Techniques such as controlled breathing and mindfulness can help keep fear in check. By focusing on the present moment and breaking down challenges into manageable tasks, you can prevent fear from overwhelming your thought process.

Consider the story of Aron Ralston, who became famous for his harrowing experience in a Utah canyon. Trapped by a boulder that had pinned his arm, he faced a seemingly impossible situation. Ralston's will to survive was evident in his methodical approach to problem-solving. He assessed his situation, rationed his limited resources, and, ultimately, made the excruciating decision to amputate his own arm to free himself. His story is a testament to the power of mental fortitude and the human spirit's capacity to endure unimaginable hardship.

Staying optimistic is another crucial component of the will to survive. Optimism doesn't mean ignoring the gravity of your situation; rather, it involves maintaining hope and believing in the possibility of rescue or finding a way out. This positive mindset can significantly impact your ability to persevere. Studies have shown that individuals with a hopeful outlook are more likely to engage in proactive behavior, which can lead to better outcomes in survival scenarios.

Take the example of the soccer team trapped in the Tham Luang cave in Thailand. Despite being stuck underground for over two weeks, the boys and their coach maintained a hopeful attitude, which was critical in conserving their energy and staying calm. Their belief in rescue, combined with their coach's guidance in meditation and breathing techniques, helped them endure the ordeal until help arrived.

In addition to optimism, setting small, achievable goals can bolster your will to survive. When faced with a daunting situation, breaking it down into smaller, manageable tasks can provide a sense of progress and accomplishment. These micro-goals serve as stepping stones, keeping you motivated and focused.

Imagine you're lost at sea on a lifeboat. The vastness of the ocean can be overwhelming, and the uncertainty of rescue can be demoralizing. By setting small goals, such as collecting rainwater, catching fish, or maintaining the lifeboat, you create a routine that structures your day and gives you purpose. These tasks not only increase your chances of survival but also keep your mind engaged and your spirit resilient.

Another vital aspect of the will to survive is adaptability. Survival situations are often unpredictable, requiring you to think on your feet and adjust your plans as circumstances change. Flexibility in your approach can prevent you from becoming fixated on a single solution, which might not be feasible.

Consider the experience of Yossi Ghinsberg, who was lost in the Amazon rainforest. Initially, he had a plan to follow the river to find civilization. However, when he encountered impassable rapids, he had to change his strategy. Ghinsberg adapted by finding alternative routes and using his surroundings to his advantage, demonstrating that survival often depends on your ability to pivot and innovate.

Social connections and the support of others can also significantly enhance your will to survive. If you're with a group, fostering a sense of camaraderie and mutual support can be incredibly powerful. Humans are inherently social creatures, and the presence of others can provide emotional comfort, share the workload, and offer different perspectives on solving problems.

In group survival scenarios, effective communication is critical. Sharing your thoughts, fears, and ideas openly can strengthen the group's cohesion. For example, during the ill-fated expedition of the Endurance, Ernest Shackleton's leadership and his crew's solidarity were pivotal. Despite being stranded on the Antarctic ice for months, their unwavering support for each other and Shackleton's optimistic leadership kept their spirits high and ultimately led to their rescue.

Even in solitary survival situations, the mental image of loved ones and the desire to reunite with them can fuel your will to survive. The thought of family and friends provides a powerful emotional anchor, reminding you of what you're fighting for. Many survivors recount how the hope of seeing their loved ones again gave them the strength to endure extreme hardships.

Another key element in the will to survive is resourcefulness. Making the most of available resources and improvising with what you have can be lifesaving. In survival situations, ingenuity can turn seemingly useless objects into vital tools. This resourcefulness not only addresses practical needs but also reinforces your sense of control and capability.

For instance, Les Stroud, known as Survivorman, emphasizes the importance of creativity in survival. In one of his episodes, stranded in a remote area with limited supplies, he used shoelaces to create traps and fashioned a fishing spear from a tree branch. His ability to see potential in ordinary items exemplifies how resourcefulness can sustain you physically and mentally.

Lastly, spiritual beliefs and practices can play a significant role in sustaining the will to survive. For some, faith in a higher power or a sense of purpose beyond oneself can provide strength and comfort. Whether through prayer, meditation, or other spiritual practices, connecting with something greater can offer solace and hope in dire circumstances.

In summary, the will to survive is a multifaceted blend of mental resilience, optimism, goal-setting, adaptability, social support, resourcefulness, and, for some, spiritual faith. Cultivating these elements can dramatically improve your chances of enduring and overcoming extreme situations. By understanding and harnessing the power of the human spirit, you can face survival challenges with a fortified heart and an unwavering determination to prevail.

Finding and Purifying Water in the Wild

Water is the essence of life, and in a survival situation, finding and purifying water becomes a top priority. Without it, the human body can only last a few days, and dehydration can quickly lead to severe health complications. This chapter explores practical methods for locating water sources in the wild and ensuring that the water you drink is safe and free from harmful pathogens.

First and foremost, understanding the landscape is crucial when searching for water. Natural indicators, such as the presence of lush vegetation, can often signal the proximity of water. Valleys and low-lying areas tend to collect water runoff, making them prime spots to search. Animals and insects also serve as valuable guides. For instance, observing animal tracks or bird flight patterns can lead you to water. Birds, particularly those that feed on aquatic life, often travel to and from water sources at dawn and dusk.

When venturing into the wild, it's wise to carry a map and compass to navigate effectively. Topographic maps, in particular, can reveal the presence of rivers, streams, and lakes. If you find yourself without such tools, the sun and stars can help determine direction. In the northern hemisphere, moss tends to grow on the north side of trees, where it's cooler and shadier, providing another clue for orientation.

Once you locate a potential water source, ensuring its purity is paramount. Even crystal-clear water can harbor harmful microorganisms, such as bacteria, viruses, and parasites. Drinking untreated water can lead to illnesses like giardiasis and dysentery. Therefore, purification should never be overlooked.

Boiling water is one of the most effective methods to kill pathogens. By bringing water to a rolling boil for at least one minute, you can eliminate most harmful organisms. At higher altitudes, where water boils at lower temperatures, extending the boiling time to three minutes is advisable. While boiling is highly effective, it requires a heat source and a container, which might not always be available.

In such cases, chemical purification methods can serve as a reliable alternative. Water purification tablets, commonly containing chlorine dioxide or iodine, are lightweight and easy to carry. When using these tablets, follow the manufacturer's instructions carefully, as the effectiveness depends on the correct dosage and contact time. Although chemical treatments are generally effective, they can leave an unpleasant taste. This can be mitigated by adding flavored drink mixes after the purification process.

For those looking to avoid the taste of chemicals, filtration systems offer another viable option. Portable water filters, such as pump filters or straw filters, are designed to remove bacteria and protozoa. Some advanced models can even filter out viruses. When using a filter, ensure that it's rated for the specific contaminants present in the water source. Filters with a pore size of 0.1 microns or smaller are generally effective against most pathogens.

In scenarios where you lack access to boiling equipment, chemical tablets, or a filtration system, natural purification methods can be employed. One such method is solar disinfection, or SODIS. This technique involves filling a clear plastic bottle with water and exposing it to direct sunlight for at least six hours. The ultraviolet rays from the sun can kill many harmful microorganisms. For best results, use PET bottles and shake the water vigorously to oxygenate it before placing it in the sun.

Another natural method involves the use of improvised filters. Creating a simple filter from materials found in the wild can help remove debris and some pathogens. Start by layering sand, charcoal, and small pebbles in a container, allowing water to pass through each layer. While this method doesn't guarantee complete purification, it can significantly reduce the number of contaminants.

In addition to these methods, understanding how to collect water from less obvious sources can be lifesaving. Dew collection, for instance, is a valuable technique, especially in arid environments. By tying absorbent cloths to your ankles and walking through tall grass at dawn, you can gather dew, which can then be wrung out into a container. Similarly, rainwater collection is straightforward and generally safe to drink. Use large leaves, tarps, or any concave surface to channel rainwater into a container.

Transpiration bags offer another innovative way to collect water. By placing a plastic bag over a leafy branch and sealing it around the stem, you can capture water vapor released by the plant through transpiration. Over time, the vapor condenses inside the bag, providing a small but steady supply of water.

This method works best with non-toxic plants and requires patience, as the process can take several hours.

In coastal regions, desalination might be necessary to make seawater drinkable. While boiling seawater and capturing the condensed steam is effective, it requires specific equipment and time. Simpler methods, like using a solar still, can also be employed. To create a solar still, dig a hole in the ground, place a container in the center, and cover the hole with plastic sheeting. Secure the edges with rocks and place a small stone in the center of the plastic, directly above the container. As the sun heats the ground, water vapor will condense on the plastic and drip into the container, providing fresh water.

While finding and purifying water is essential, so is conserving it. In a survival situation, every drop counts. Avoid strenuous activity during the hottest parts of the day to reduce sweat loss, and seek shade whenever possible. Ration your water carefully, and remember that food intake increases your body's need for water. If supplies are limited, prioritize hydration over eating.

Mental fortitude also plays a significant role in managing water scarcity. Dehydration can impair cognitive function, making it harder to think clearly and make sound decisions. Staying calm and focused, even when water is scarce, can help you manage your resources more effectively and avoid unnecessary risks.

In conclusion, mastering the art of finding and purifying water in the wild is a critical survival skill. By understanding the landscape, using natural indicators, and employing a variety of purification methods, you can secure a safe water supply in even the most challenging environments. Remember, preparation and knowledge are your best allies in any survival situation. Equip yourself with the right tools and techniques,

and you'll be better prepared to face the wild with confidence
and resilience.

Fire Starting Techniques

Fire has been a cornerstone of human survival for millennia, providing warmth, light, protection, and a means to cook food and purify water. In the wild, knowing how to start a fire can be a game-changer, transforming a dire situation into a manageable one. This chapter delves into various fire-starting techniques that are essential for anyone venturing into the wilderness.

Imagine you're deep in the forest as the sun begins to set. The temperature drops rapidly, and the need for a fire becomes urgent. The first step in any fire-starting process is gathering the necessary materials. Tinder, kindling, and fuel are the three critical components. Tinder is the smallest and most combustible material, such as dry grass, leaves, or birch bark. It catches fire easily and burns quickly. Kindling consists of small sticks and twigs that catch fire from the tinder and burn long enough to ignite the larger fuel logs.

When collecting these materials, always ensure they are dry. Wet or damp materials will make the fire-starting process significantly more challenging. One useful technique is to look for tinder and kindling in sheltered areas, such as under overhangs or inside hollow logs, where they are less likely to be wet.

One of the most reliable fire-starting tools is the classic match. However, matches can become useless if they get wet or the striker strip gets damaged. Therefore, waterproof matches or storing regular matches in a waterproof container is highly recommended. If matches are unavailable, a lighter is another dependable option. But, like matches, it can fail if it gets wet or runs out of fuel.

For those who prefer a more traditional approach, the flint and steel method is worth mastering. Striking a steel striker against a piece of flint generates sparks that can ignite tinder. The key to success with flint and steel is to strike with enough force to produce a shower of sparks while holding the flint at the right angle. Practice is essential to become proficient with this technique.

Modern alternatives, such as ferrocerium rods (ferro rods), are highly effective and durable. Unlike flint and steel, which rely on natural materials, ferro rods are man-made and produce a much hotter spark. To use a ferro rod, scrape the rod with a metal striker or the back of a knife blade, directing the sparks onto the tinder. The intense sparks can ignite even slightly damp tinder, making ferro rods a valuable tool in adverse conditions.

In a pinch, using a magnifying glass or a lens from a camera or binoculars can harness solar power to start a fire. This method requires direct sunlight and patience. Focus the sunlight into a small point on the tinder, holding it steady until the tinder begins to smolder. Once you see smoke, gently blow on the tinder to encourage it to catch fire. While this technique is effective under the right conditions, it is limited to sunny days and requires steady hands.

The bow drill is another primitive, yet effective, fire-starting method. It involves creating friction between a spindle and a fireboard. To construct a bow drill, you'll need a sturdy stick for the spindle, a flat piece of wood for the fireboard, a curved piece of wood with a string for the bow, and a socket to hold the spindle in place. The spindle is spun rapidly against the fireboard using the bow, generating heat through friction until the tinder catches fire. Mastering the bow drill requires practice and patience, but it is a valuable skill when modern tools are unavailable.

Chemical fire starters, such as potassium permanganate and glycerin, can also be used to start a fire. When these two substances are mixed, they react exothermically, producing enough heat to ignite tinder. However, handling chemicals requires caution and knowledge. Always follow safety guidelines and use this method only if you are confident in your understanding of the materials.

Once you have successfully ignited your tinder, it's crucial to nurture the flame. Gently add small pieces of kindling to the growing flame, gradually increasing the size of the sticks. Avoid smothering the flame by adding too much material too quickly. Instead, build the fire slowly and steadily, allowing each layer to catch fire before adding more.

Creating a fire structure can significantly enhance your fire-starting success. The teepee, lean-to, and log cabin are three common fire structures. The teepee involves arranging the kindling in a conical shape around the tinder, allowing air to circulate and feed the flame. The lean-to structure uses a larger log or stick as a support, with smaller sticks leaning against it, creating a shelter for the tinder and kindling. The log cabin involves stacking sticks in a square formation around the tinder, providing a stable base for the fire.

In wet or damp conditions, starting a fire can be particularly challenging. One technique to overcome this is to use a base of dry materials to keep the tinder off the cold, wet ground. Birch bark, which burns even when wet, can be an excellent tinder choice in such conditions. Additionally, using a small piece of cotton ball soaked in petroleum jelly can provide a reliable and long-lasting flame to ignite damp kindling.

It's important to remember that fire safety is paramount. Always clear the area around your fire of any flammable materials and never leave a fire unattended. When extinguishing a fire, ensure it is completely out by dousing it with water and stirring the ashes until they are cool to the touch. This prevents accidental wildfires and ensures the safety of the environment and yourself.

In survival situations, the ability to start a fire can mean the difference between life and death. Whether you're using modern tools like matches and lighters or traditional methods like flint and steel or the bow drill, practice and preparation are key. Familiarize yourself with multiple fire-starting techniques and carry the necessary tools whenever you venture into the wild. By mastering these skills, you'll be better prepared to face any challenge nature throws your way, transforming uncertainty into confidence and survival into success.

When you find yourself in the wild, one of the most immediate concerns is protection from the elements. A well-built shelter can provide the warmth, safety, and comfort needed to survive and thrive in nature. Knowing how to construct various types of shelters, depending on the environment and available materials, is a critical skill. This chapter will guide you through the construction of different shelters, ensuring you can adapt to any situation.

Imagine you're deep in a dense forest, the sky darkening as a storm approaches. The need for a shelter becomes pressing. The first step is to assess your surroundings and gather the necessary materials. Your choice of shelter will depend on the weather conditions, available resources, and the time you have.

The simplest and quickest form of shelter is the debris hut. This shelter requires minimal tools and can be constructed from natural materials found almost anywhere. Start by finding a ridgepole – a sturdy branch or log about your height. Prop one end up on a tree stump, rock, or forked branch about your chest height, and let the other end rest on the ground. This creates the backbone of your shelter. Next, lean smaller sticks against both sides of the ridgepole, forming a frame that resembles a small A-frame house. Cover this frame with layers of leaves, grass, and other debris to insulate and keep out rain. Ensure the debris is thick, at least a foot deep, to provide adequate protection. Finally, pile more debris on the ground inside the shelter for bedding.

In colder climates or snowy conditions, the snow cave is an excellent option. Snow caves provide excellent insulation and can be surprisingly warm inside. To build one, find a snowdrift or a deep snowbank. Dig an entrance that slopes upward into a small chamber, ensuring you dig out a ventilation hole to prevent suffocation. The ceiling of your snow cave should be dome-shaped to prevent dripping and for structural integrity. Smooth the interior walls to reduce the risk of collapse and to reflect body heat back into the chamber. Remember, building a snow cave is labor-intensive and should only be undertaken if you have the energy and time.

If you are in a desert or arid environment, protection from the sun is paramount. A simple sunshade can be constructed using a tarp, poncho, or even large pieces of clothing. Stretch the material between two points, such as rocks or bushes, to create a shaded area. If no natural tie points are available, you can use sticks driven into the ground. Ensure the shaded area allows for airflow underneath to keep cool. In deserts, digging a shallow trench to lie in can also help reduce exposure to the sun and wind.

For those in coastal or beach environments, a driftwood shelter can be both effective and quick to construct. Search for large pieces of driftwood or fallen branches and arrange them in a lean-to structure against a rock, sand dune, or cliff. Cover the structure with seaweed, grass, or other available materials to provide insulation and protection from the wind. Coastal areas often have abundant natural materials, making this type of shelter relatively easy to build.

In tropical regions, the elevated jungle lean-to is ideal for keeping you off the wet ground and away from insects and small animals. Start by finding two sturdy trees about six to eight feet apart. Lash a horizontal pole between them at waist height. Lean long sticks or bamboo poles against this horizontal pole to form a slanted roof. Cover the roof with large leaves, palm fronds, or any available vegetation to create a waterproof layer. Elevate your sleeping area by lashing more poles horizontally between the trees, about two feet off the ground, and cover these poles with leaves or a groundsheet if you have one.

For those who have more time and resources, the log cabin or wickiup can provide a more permanent and sturdy shelter. A log cabin requires significant labor and tools but offers excellent protection and durability. Start by selecting straight logs and cutting them to the desired length. Lay the logs in a square or rectangular shape, notching the ends so they fit together securely. Continue stacking logs, alternating the notches at each corner, until the walls reach the desired height. Leave space for a doorway and, if possible, windows. Cover the roof with more logs or branches and insulate with moss, leaves, or other materials.

The wickiup, traditionally used by Native American tribes, is a dome-shaped structure made from flexible branches. Gather long, flexible branches and stick them into the ground in a circular pattern, bending and tying them together at the top to form a dome. Weave smaller branches horizontally through the vertical ones to create a sturdy frame. Cover the frame with grass, reeds, or bark to insulate and protect from the elements. The wickiup is particularly effective in temperate climates and can be built relatively quickly with the right materials.

In all shelter-building scenarios, location is crucial. Choose a site that is dry, flat, and free from hazards such as falling branches or flooding. Avoid setting up near water sources where insects are more prevalent and where predators may come to drink. Look for natural windbreaks like large rocks or dense vegetation to protect your shelter from the wind.

Fire can be a valuable addition to your shelter, providing warmth, light, and protection. Build your fire outside the entrance of your shelter, ensuring it is far enough away to prevent sparks from reaching the structure. Reflective walls or rocks behind the fire can help direct heat into the shelter, increasing its efficiency.

Survival is as much about mental resilience as it is about physical skills. Building a shelter not only protects you from the elements but also provides a psychological boost, giving you a sense of security and control in a challenging environment. Practice these shelter-building techniques in different environments to gain confidence and proficiency.

Preparation is key. Equip yourself with basic tools like a knife, cordage, and a tarp, which can significantly ease the shelter-building process. Knowledge and practice will transform these techniques into instinctual responses, ensuring you can adapt and survive in any situation. Whether you find yourself in a dense forest, snowy mountains, scorching desert, or tropical jungle, understanding how to construct a variety of shelters is an essential survival skill.

Accidents and injuries are inevitable in the wilderness, making basic first aid knowledge an essential survival skill. Knowing how to treat wounds, manage pain, and stabilize injuries can make the difference between a minor inconvenience and a life-threatening situation. Understanding basic wilderness first aid helps you stay calm and effective when faced with medical emergencies far from professional help.

Imagine you're on a hiking expedition when a fellow hiker suddenly slips on a loose rock, tumbling down a slope. The immediate response is crucial. First, ensure the scene is safe for both the injured person and yourself. Approach carefully, assessing any potential hazards like unstable ground or falling rocks. Once you reach the injured hiker, the first priority is to check their responsiveness and breathing. If they're unconscious but breathing, position them into the recovery position to keep their airway open. If they're not breathing, initiate CPR immediately while sending someone to get help if possible.

For conscious individuals, conduct a quick yet thorough assessment of their condition. Check for any obvious signs of injury, such as bleeding, deformities, or swelling. In the wilderness, stopping bleeding is critical. Use a clean cloth or a piece of your clothing to apply direct pressure to the wound. Elevate the injured area above heart level if possible, and secure the dressing with a bandage or another piece of cloth. If the bleeding doesn't stop after applying pressure, consider using a tourniquet as a last resort, placing it above the wound and tightening until the bleeding stops.

Wounds in the wild can easily become infected due to the abundance of bacteria. Cleaning the wound thoroughly is vital. Use clean water to rinse out dirt and debris, and if you have an antiseptic solution, apply it to the wound. Cover the cleaned wound with a sterile bandage or the cleanest material you have available. Change the dressing daily and monitor for signs of infection, such as redness, swelling, or pus.

Sprains and fractures are common in outdoor adventures. If you suspect a sprain, follow the RICE method: Rest, Ice, Compression, and Elevation. Rest the injured limb and avoid putting weight on it. If you have ice or a cold pack, apply it to the area to reduce swelling. Wrap the sprain with an elastic bandage to provide support and compression, but not so tightly that it cuts off circulation. Elevate the injured limb above heart level to reduce swelling.

For fractures, immobilization is key to prevent further injury. Create a splint using available materials like sticks, trekking poles, or rolled-up clothing. Place the splint along the injured limb, ensuring it extends beyond the joints above and below the fracture. Secure the splint with bandages, strips of cloth, or even shoelaces, making sure it's snug but not too tight. If the fracture is open, where the bone protrudes through the skin, cover the wound with a sterile dressing before splinting and seek immediate medical help.

Burns can occur from campfires, cooking, or even prolonged sun exposure. For minor burns, cool the affected area with clean water for at least ten minutes. Do not use ice, as it can damage the skin further. After cooling, cover the burn with a sterile, non-stick dressing or a clean cloth. Avoid applying creams or ointments, as these can trap heat in the skin. For more severe burns, seek immediate medical assistance, and if possible, cover the burn with a clean, moist dressing to prevent infection.

Hypothermia and heat exhaustion are serious conditions that require immediate attention. Hypothermia occurs when the body loses heat faster than it can produce it, leading to a dangerously low body temperature. Symptoms include shivering, confusion, and slurred speech. To treat hypothermia, move the person to a warmer environment, remove any wet clothing, and wrap them in dry blankets or clothing. Provide warm, non-alcoholic, and non-caffeinated beverages if they're conscious and able to swallow.

Heat exhaustion results from excessive heat and dehydration. Symptoms include heavy sweating, weakness, dizziness, and nausea. Move the person to a shaded or cooler area, have them lie down, and elevate their legs. Encourage them to drink water or a rehydration solution. Apply cool, wet cloths to their skin or fan them to help lower their body temperature. If untreated, heat exhaustion can progress to heat stroke, a life-threatening condition that requires immediate medical attention.

Insect bites and stings are common in the wilderness and can range from annoying to dangerous, especially for those with allergies. For most bites and stings, clean the area with soap and water and apply a cold pack to reduce swelling. If the person shows signs of an allergic reaction, such as difficulty breathing, swelling of the face or throat, or hives, administer an epinephrine auto-injector if available and seek emergency help immediately.

Dehydration is another common issue that can have serious consequences. Symptoms include dizziness, dark urine, and extreme thirst. Prevent dehydration by drinking water regularly, even if you don't feel thirsty. If you suspect dehydration, have the person rest in a shaded area and sip water slowly. Electrolyte solutions or oral rehydration salts can help restore balance more effectively than plain water.

Poisoning from plants, berries, or contaminated water is a risk in the wild. Familiarize yourself with the local flora and avoid consuming anything you're not sure is safe. If poisoning is suspected, try to identify the source and seek medical help immediately. Do not induce vomiting unless advised by a medical professional. Keep the person hydrated and monitor their symptoms closely.

In all wilderness first aid scenarios, communication and planning are crucial. Always inform someone of your plans before heading into the wilderness and have a means of communication, such as a satellite phone or emergency beacon, in case of emergencies. Carry a well-stocked first aid kit, tailored to the specific environment and potential risks. Include items like bandages, antiseptics, pain relievers, tweezers, scissors, and a first aid manual. Regularly check and replenish your kit to ensure it's ready when needed.

Being prepared and knowledgeable about first aid can make a significant difference in the outcome of wilderness emergencies. Practice these skills and stay calm in the face of adversity. Your ability to respond effectively can save lives and make your wilderness adventures safer and more enjoyable.

Lost in the wilderness without a map or compass, the situation might seem dire, but nature provides numerous clues to help you find your way. Understanding how to navigate using natural indicators can be a lifesaver. This chapter delves into practical techniques and strategies for finding your direction and reaching safety, relying solely on environmental cues.

Imagine you're hiking in a dense forest, and you realize you've veered off the trail. Panic sets in, but taking a moment to calm yourself is the first step toward effective navigation. Your initial goal should be to determine the cardinal directions—north, south, east, and west. One simple method is to observe the position of the sun. In the Northern Hemisphere, the sun rises in the east and sets in the west. Around midday, it's generally in the southern part of the sky. By noting the sun's position at different times of the day, you can estimate the cardinal directions.

If the sun isn't visible, other natural indicators can assist. Trees often provide clues; in the Northern Hemisphere, moss tends to grow thicker on the north side of trees due to reduced sunlight. However, this isn't foolproof, as local conditions can affect moss growth. Additionally, tree branches are usually denser on the south side because they receive more sunlight. When using these indicators, it's best to find a pattern rather than relying on a single tree.

Shadows can also guide you. The shadow-tip method involves placing a stick vertically in the ground and marking the tip of its shadow with a rock or another marker. Wait about fifteen minutes and mark the new position of the shadow tip. Draw a straight line between the two marks; this line roughly runs west to east, with the first mark indicating west.

At night, the stars become your navigational allies. The North Star, or Polaris, is a reliable indicator of north in the Northern Hemisphere. Locate the Big Dipper constellation and use the two stars on the outer edge of its "bowl" to point directly to Polaris. In the Southern Hemisphere, find the Southern Cross constellation. Extend an imaginary line along its long axis to approximate the direction of the south celestial pole.

Natural landmarks are invaluable for maintaining your bearings. Rivers, mountains, and valleys can serve as guideposts. Rivers generally flow in a single direction and often lead to human settlements. If you follow a river downstream, you're likely to encounter roads or inhabited areas. Mountains and ridges can be used to orient yourself; in many regions, they run in a particular direction, such as north-south or east-west. By understanding the general layout of the land, you can use these features to navigate.

Animal behavior can also provide hints about direction. Birds often fly toward water sources in the morning and return to their nests in the evening. Observing these patterns can help you locate water, which is crucial for survival and can lead to human habitation. Insects like ants often build their nests on the south side of trees and rocks to take advantage of the warmth, offering another subtle clue.

In open areas, wind patterns can be a guide. Wind generally blows from predictable directions depending on the season and geography. Understanding local wind patterns can help you determine your direction of travel. For instance, in many coastal areas, sea breezes blow inland during the day and reverse at night.

When traveling without a map or compass, it's essential to establish a reference point and use it to gauge your progress. Choose a distant landmark, such as a mountain peak or a distinctive tree, and keep it in view as you move. This strategy helps you maintain a straight line of travel and prevents you from walking in circles, which is a common mistake when lost.

If you find yourself completely disoriented, it's often best to stay put and wait for rescue, especially if you've informed someone of your plans and expected return. Building a signal fire or creating large ground signals with rocks or branches can increase your visibility to search parties or aircraft.

In survival situations, your mental state is as crucial as your physical condition. Staying calm and thinking logically will improve your decision-making abilities. Regularly assess your situation, resources, and surroundings to make informed choices. Hydration and energy conservation are vital; avoid excessive exertion during the hottest parts of the day and ration your water supply.

Creating a daily routine can help maintain morale and structure. Plan your movements during the cooler parts of the day, such as early morning or late afternoon. Use midday for rest and shelter building. This approach conserves energy and reduces the risk of heat exhaustion.

Navigation skills improve with practice, so take opportunities to hone them. Practice using the sun, stars, and natural landmarks to find your way, even when you're not lost. Familiarize yourself with the local flora, fauna, and geological features of areas you visit. The more you know about your environment, the better equipped you'll be to navigate it.

Proper preparation can prevent many navigation issues. Always inform someone of your plans and expected return time before heading into the wilderness. Carry basic survival gear, including a whistle, mirror, and a portable GPS device, if possible. These tools can significantly increase your chances of being found if you do get lost.

Understanding how to navigate without a map and compass transforms a potentially life-threatening situation into a manageable challenge. By observing natural indicators, maintaining a calm and logical mindset, and practicing your skills regularly, you can confidently explore and enjoy the wilderness. The knowledge that you can find your way using the environment around you is empowering and enhances your overall outdoor experience.

Navigating Urban Disasters

In the midst of an urban disaster, chaos often reigns supreme. Whether it's an earthquake, a flood, a terrorist attack, or a prolonged power outage, navigating the complexities of a city suddenly plunged into crisis requires a blend of preparedness, adaptability, and presence of mind. This chapter provides essential strategies for safely maneuvering through an urban environment during a disaster, helping you stay safe and find your way amidst the turmoil.

Picture this: It's a typical weekday morning, and the city is bustling with activity. Suddenly, the ground begins to shake violently. Buildings sway, car alarms blare, and panic ensues. In the aftermath of an earthquake, your first priority is to protect yourself from immediate hazards. If you're indoors, drop to your hands and knees, cover your head and neck, and take shelter under a sturdy piece of furniture or against an interior wall away from windows. If you're outside, move away from buildings, streetlights, and utility wires. Once the shaking stops, it's time to assess your surroundings and plan your next moves.

One of the key challenges in navigating urban disasters is the potential disruption to familiar landmarks and routes. Streets may be blocked by debris, public transportation systems could be down, and communication networks might be overloaded. Therefore, it's crucial to have a mental map of your area, including alternative routes and key locations such as hospitals, police stations, and emergency shelters. If you're unfamiliar with the area, quickly orient yourself by locating major roads or landmarks.

Communication is vital, but during a disaster, traditional methods like phones and the internet may be unreliable. Establishing a pre-disaster communication plan with family and friends can save valuable time and reduce anxiety. Designate a meeting spot and a primary and secondary contact person who lives outside the affected area. This way, even if local networks are down, you can relay messages through someone who can still communicate effectively.

In the confusion following an urban disaster, misinformation can spread rapidly. Rely on trusted sources for updates and instructions. Battery-operated radios can be lifesavers, providing access to emergency broadcasts. Additionally, social media platforms can offer real-time information, but verify the credibility of the sources before acting on any advice.

Navigating through a city in crisis often involves making quick decisions about the safest routes to take. Avoid areas with high potential for secondary hazards, such as bridges, tunnels, and waterfronts, which may be compromised. Stick to open spaces where you can easily observe your surroundings and avoid getting trapped. If you're traveling by car, be prepared for roadblocks and traffic jams. Having a full tank of gas and an emergency kit in your vehicle can be crucial.

While moving through the city, pay close attention to your environment. Listen for sounds that might indicate danger, such as creaking structures or sirens, and watch for visual cues like smoke or unstable buildings. Trust your instincts; if something feels unsafe, find an alternative path. Stay calm and move deliberately—panic can lead to poor decisions and increase your risk.

Personal safety is paramount. In the aftermath of a disaster, crime rates can spike as law enforcement resources are stretched thin. Avoid isolated areas and travel in groups if possible. Keep a low profile, and do not display valuables that might attract unwanted attention. Self-defense tools like pepper spray can provide an added layer of security, but their use should be considered within the context of local laws and personal safety training.

Disasters can create a range of medical emergencies, from cuts and bruises to more severe injuries. Basic first aid knowledge is invaluable. Carry a first aid kit and be familiar with its contents. If someone is injured, provide immediate care to the best of your ability and seek professional medical help as soon as possible. Remember the principles of first aid: stop bleeding, protect wounds, immobilize injured limbs, and prevent shock.

Water and food supplies may become scarce during an urban disaster. Store at least three days' worth of non-perishable food and water for each member of your household. Water purification tablets and portable filters can make contaminated water safe to drink. Knowing where to find emergency supplies in your city—such as community centers or designated emergency distribution points—can also help you access necessities.

Shelter is another critical consideration. If your home is unsafe, identify alternative locations where you can stay. Public shelters set up by local authorities or humanitarian organizations are designed to provide safety and basic needs. However, these can become crowded, so having a personal plan for shelter, like a friend's house or a pre-identified safe building, is beneficial.

Mental resilience is as important as physical preparedness. Disasters can be traumatic, and maintaining a positive mindset helps you think clearly and make better decisions. Techniques such as deep breathing, mindfulness, and focusing on actionable steps can reduce stress. Stay connected with others, share information, and provide mutual support.

Navigating urban disasters is not just about immediate survival; it's also about long-term recovery. Once the immediate danger has passed, focus on re-establishing your routine and accessing available resources for rebuilding. Contact local authorities and relief organizations for assistance with housing, financial aid, and psychological support. Document any damage to your property for insurance claims and keep records of your interactions with service providers.

In the aftermath of a disaster, communities often come together to rebuild and support one another. Volunteering your time and skills can make a significant difference and help restore a sense of normalcy. Engaging in community efforts also connects you with others who are facing similar challenges, fostering resilience and collective strength.

Preparation is the cornerstone of navigating urban disasters. Regularly review and update your emergency plans, and participate in local disaster preparedness drills. Familiarize yourself with the potential risks in your area and take proactive steps to mitigate them, such as securing heavy furniture, installing smoke detectors, and creating an emergency supply kit. Educate your family members about these plans and ensure everyone knows what to do in different scenarios.

Ultimately, navigating urban disasters requires a combination of knowledge, preparedness, and adaptability. By understanding the risks, planning ahead, and staying informed, you can protect yourself and your loved ones in times of crisis. Embrace a proactive mindset, remain vigilant, and remember that each step you take towards preparedness strengthens your ability to navigate the unpredictable landscape of urban disasters.

Finding Safe Shelter in the City

The city hums with life and activity, a dynamic landscape of towering buildings, bustling streets, and diverse neighborhoods. Yet, in times of emergency or urban disaster, this vibrant environment can quickly become a daunting maze. Finding safe shelter amid the chaos is crucial not only for immediate survival but also for maintaining a sense of security and stability. This chapter explores practical strategies for identifying and securing safe shelter in an urban setting, ensuring you can navigate crises with confidence and resilience.

Imagine you're in the heart of the city when a severe storm suddenly strikes. The sky darkens, and the wind howls through the streets, ripping signs from buildings and sending debris flying. Seeking immediate shelter is your top priority. Ideally, you should already be aware of potential safe havens around you. Public buildings such as libraries, schools, and community centers often serve as official emergency shelters during disasters. These locations are typically well-constructed and equipped to handle large groups of people, providing both physical safety and essential services.

If you're caught outside with no public buildings nearby, look for other sturdy structures. Modern office buildings, with their reinforced construction, are generally safer than older, less stable structures. Basements and underground parking garages can offer refuge from high winds and flying debris. However, beware of flooding in these areas, especially during heavy rains. If you must take shelter in a basement, ensure you have a clear escape route should water levels rise.

In situations where you need to find shelter quickly, knowing the layout of your city can be a lifesaver. Familiarize yourself with the locations of hospitals, fire stations, and police stations. These facilities are often designed to remain operational during emergencies and can provide immediate assistance. Additionally, identify parks and open spaces that could serve as temporary safe zones, away from the danger of falling debris and collapsing structures.

Once you've secured a safe location, the next step is to ensure it remains a viable shelter. If you're indoors, check for structural damage and potential hazards such as gas leaks or exposed wiring. Block off any broken windows or doors to protect against the elements and potential intruders. If you're in a public shelter, follow the instructions of emergency personnel and participate in any organized efforts to maintain the safety and functionality of the space.

Securing safe shelter also involves considering your immediate needs and those of any companions. Ensure you have access to clean water, food, and basic medical supplies. In an emergency shelter, these resources are typically provided, but it's wise to have your emergency kit stocked with essentials. This kit should include bottled water, non-perishable food, a first aid kit, flashlight, batteries, and any necessary medications.

In the event of a prolonged crisis, creating a sense of normalcy within your shelter can greatly enhance your ability to cope. Establish routines for meals, rest, and personal hygiene. Engage in activities that provide mental stimulation and help pass the time, such as reading, playing games, or practicing mindfulness exercises. Maintaining a positive mindset and staying occupied can reduce stress and improve your overall well-being.

Community cooperation is vital in urban shelters. Working together with others can enhance safety and resource management. Share information and resources, assist with communal tasks, and support those who may be more vulnerable, such as the elderly or those with disabilities. A strong sense of community can foster resilience and create a more supportive environment for everyone involved.

While public shelters and designated safe zones are often the best option during large-scale emergencies, there are times when you may need to create your own shelter. If you're forced to evacuate your home and can't reach an official shelter, knowing how to improvise can be crucial. Look for buildings that are structurally sound and offer protection from the elements. Avoid places with large windows or flat roofs, which are more susceptible to wind damage and collapse.

When constructing an improvised shelter, prioritize safety and stability. Use available materials to reinforce doors and windows, and create barriers against wind and rain. If you have access to tools and supplies, consider building a more robust structure using wood, metal, or other durable materials. Ensure your shelter has ventilation and a means of escape in case conditions worsen.

During cold weather, finding or creating a warm shelter is essential to prevent hypothermia. Insulate your space using blankets, clothing, and any other materials at hand. If you have a portable stove or heater, use it safely and ensure proper ventilation to avoid carbon monoxide poisoning. In hot weather, seek shade and create airflow to prevent heat exhaustion and dehydration. Stay hydrated by drinking water regularly and avoiding strenuous activities during the hottest parts of the day.

Pets are part of the family and should be included in your shelter plans. Ensure you have food, water, and any necessary medications for your pets. Keep them close to reduce their stress and prevent them from running away or getting lost. Many public shelters have provisions for pets, but it's always best to be prepared with your own supplies.

Urban shelters can become crowded, and maintaining hygiene is critical to prevent the spread of illness. Wash your hands regularly, use hand sanitizer, and dispose of waste properly. If possible, designate specific areas for eating, sleeping, and using the restroom to minimize contamination. In a prolonged crisis, sanitation can become a significant concern, so plan ahead to manage waste and maintain cleanliness.

Communication remains a cornerstone of safety in an urban shelter. Stay informed about the situation outside by listening to emergency broadcasts on a battery-operated radio. Share updates with others in your shelter and coordinate efforts to address any challenges that arise. If you're in contact with family or friends outside the affected area, keep them informed of your status and any changes in your situation.

As the immediate danger subsides and the city begins to recover, transition from emergency sheltering to more stable living conditions. Assess the safety of your home or other long-term housing options before returning. If your home is damaged, seek assistance from local authorities and relief organizations to secure temporary housing and begin the rebuilding process. Document any damage for insurance claims and keep records of any expenses related to the disaster.

Preparation is key to successfully navigating the challenges of finding safe shelter in the city. Regularly review and update your emergency plans, and participate in local preparedness drills. Familiarize yourself with the risks specific to your area and take steps to mitigate them, such as securing heavy furniture, installing emergency lighting, and creating a family communication plan. Educate your family members about these plans and ensure everyone knows what to do in different scenarios.

Ultimately, finding safe shelter in the city during a disaster requires a combination of knowledge, preparation, and adaptability. By understanding the potential risks, planning ahead, and staying informed, you can protect yourself and your loved ones in times of crisis. Embrace a proactive mindset, remain vigilant, and remember that each step you take towards preparedness strengthens your ability to navigate the unpredictable landscape of urban disasters.

Locating Food and Water in Urban Areas

Urban environments, with their dense populations and complex infrastructures, present unique challenges when it comes to locating food and water during emergencies. Whether you're dealing with a natural disaster, a prolonged power outage, or a disruption in supply chains, understanding how to secure these essential resources can be a matter of survival. This chapter delves into practical strategies for finding and ensuring a steady supply of food and water in urban areas, focusing on methods that are accessible, sustainable, and safe.

Imagine a sudden crisis that disrupts your city's normal flow of goods. Supermarket shelves empty quickly, and the usual convenience of grabbing groceries becomes a distant memory. In such scenarios, knowing alternative sources of food is crucial. Start by pinpointing local resources. Urban areas often have community gardens, farmers' markets, and food cooperatives. These places not only offer fresh produce but also tend to be more resilient during supply chain disruptions because they rely on local growers and producers.

Community gardens can be a lifeline. These green spaces, tended by local residents, often produce a variety of fruits, vegetables, and herbs. Get involved with your nearest community garden or at least familiarize yourself with its location and operation hours. In times of need, these gardens may distribute food to the community or allow you to participate in the harvest. Establishing a connection with these gardens before an emergency can ensure you have access to fresh produce when it's most needed.

Farmers' markets are another excellent source of fresh food. These markets usually operate on specific days and offer a range of locally grown or produced items. Keep track of the market schedules and build relationships with vendors. During a crisis, these farmers might be more willing to help regular customers. Additionally, some urban farmers' markets accept SNAP benefits, making them accessible to more people.

When traditional retail options fail, food cooperatives (co-ops) can provide an alternative. Co-ops are community-owned grocery stores that prioritize local and sustainable products. Membership in a co-op often comes with benefits like discounts and access to bulk buying options. In an emergency, co-ops might have a more robust supply chain due to their local focus and community support.

Beyond these organized resources, consider foraging as a method to find food. Urban foraging involves identifying and harvesting edible plants, fruits, and nuts that grow wild in city environments. Many cities have parks and green belts where wild edibles can be found. Learn to identify common urban edibles such as dandelions, clover, and fruit-bearing trees. However, always exercise caution: avoid plants near busy roads or industrial areas due to potential contamination, and make sure you correctly identify any plant before consuming it to avoid poisoning.

Water, the most critical resource, can also be challenging to secure in an urban emergency. The first step is to assess your immediate sources. Tap water might still be running, but it may not be safe to drink without treatment. Have a supply of water purification tablets or a portable filter on hand. Boiling water is another effective method to kill pathogens, though it requires a heat source and time.

If tap water is unavailable or unsafe, look for alternative sources. Rainwater harvesting can be a viable option, particularly in cities with frequent rainfall. Use clean containers to collect and store rainwater, then treat it before drinking. Urban environments also have hidden water sources such as water heaters and toilet tanks (not the bowl). These can provide emergency water, but ensure to treat the water appropriately.

Public buildings often have emergency water supplies. Schools, government buildings, and large office complexes typically store water for emergencies. Knowing the locations of these buildings can be crucial. In a crisis, authorities may open these facilities to the public or distribute their resources.

Another strategy is to stockpile water and non-perishable food before a crisis hits. Aim to have at least a two-week supply for each family member. Store water in clean, food-grade containers, and keep them in a cool, dark place. Rotate your stock periodically to ensure freshness. Non-perishable foods like canned goods, dried beans, rice, and pasta can be stored for long periods without refrigeration. Include a manual can opener in your supplies, and consider foods that require minimal preparation.

In prolonged emergencies, you might need to think about sustainable ways to produce your own food. Urban gardening, even on a small scale, can supplement your food supply. Utilize balconies, rooftops, and windowsills to grow herbs, vegetables, and small fruit plants. Container gardening is an efficient way to maximize limited space. Learn about vertical gardening techniques, which allow you to grow more plants in smaller areas by stacking planters or using trellises.

Hydroponics and aquaponics are advanced methods that can be particularly effective in urban settings. Hydroponics involves growing plants in a nutrient-rich water solution without soil, making it suitable for indoor spaces. Aquaponics combines hydroponics with aquaculture, where fish and plants are grown together in a symbiotic environment. These systems can be set up in small indoor spaces and provide a continuous cycle of fresh produce and fish.

Community kitchens and food-sharing networks can also play a vital role. During crises, these networks often mobilize to provide meals and distribute food. Volunteering with or staying connected to such organizations can ensure you have access to communal resources. They also offer a platform to share your surplus and receive help when needed.

Lastly, always stay informed. Government agencies, local news, and community groups will provide updates on food and water distribution points during emergencies. Social media and neighborhood apps can be useful for real-time information and coordination with neighbors. Being part of a community network increases your chances of receiving timely help and sharing resources.

Preparing for urban food and water scarcity requires a combination of foresight, local knowledge, and community involvement. By familiarizing yourself with local food sources, learning basic foraging skills, and developing sustainable practices, you can enhance your resilience in the face of urban emergencies. Remember, the key to survival in any crisis is not just having resources but knowing how to find and manage them effectively. Stay proactive, build relationships, and continuously educate yourself to ensure that you and your loved ones remain safe and nourished, no matter what challenges arise.

Urban environments, with their dense populations and unique challenges, require specific self-defense techniques tailored to the complexities of city life. Navigating crowded streets, public transportation, and various urban settings demands a heightened awareness and a set of skills that can help you protect yourself and others. This chapter explores practical and actionable urban self-defense techniques, emphasizing the importance of awareness, physical readiness, and strategic thinking.

Imagine you're walking home late at night through a busy but dimly lit street. The hum of distant traffic is the only sound, and your footsteps echo slightly as you navigate the uneven pavement. Suddenly, you sense someone following you. The first and most crucial element in urban self-defense is awareness. Being aware of your surroundings can often prevent a potential threat from escalating. This means not only observing physical surroundings but also being attuned to the behavior of the people around you.

One key to maintaining awareness is to avoid distractions. In an age where smartphones are omnipresent, it's easy to become engrossed in a screen and oblivious to your environment. Make a habit of keeping your phone in your pocket and periodically scanning your surroundings. Look for exits, note the presence of security cameras, and be aware of any individuals who seem out of place or overly interested in you.

Once you have cultivated a habit of awareness, the next step is to project confidence. Attackers are often opportunists who seek out easy targets. By walking with purpose, making eye contact, and keeping an upright posture, you signal that you are not an easy victim. Confidence can deter many would-be attackers before they even make a move.

However, awareness and confidence are not always enough. Knowing basic physical self-defense techniques is essential. These techniques should be simple, effective, and easy to remember under stress. Start with the basics: striking vulnerable areas such as the eyes, nose, throat, and groin. These targets are sensitive and can incapacitate an attacker long enough for you to escape.

Learning how to break free from common holds is also crucial. For example, if someone grabs your wrist, a quick and effective technique is to rotate your wrist towards the attacker's thumb, the weakest part of their grip, and pull away sharply. If grabbed from behind, you can use a stomp to the attacker's foot, an elbow strike to the ribcage, or a headbutt to the face.

In addition to physical techniques, carrying and knowing how to use self-defense tools can provide an extra layer of security. Items such as pepper spray, personal alarms, or even a tactical flashlight can be effective deterrents. Pepper spray can incapacitate an attacker temporarily, giving you a chance to escape. Personal alarms emit a loud, piercing noise that can draw attention and scare off potential attackers. A tactical flashlight can dazzle an assailant and double as a blunt instrument if needed.

Training in a martial art can significantly enhance your self-defense capabilities. Disciplines such as Krav Maga, Brazilian Jiu-

Jitsu, and Muay Thai focus on real-world self-defense scenarios and teach techniques that are practical and effective. Regular training not only improves your physical fitness and reflexes but also builds muscle memory, making it easier to respond effectively under stress.

Situational training is another valuable component of urban self-defense. Practicing scenarios such as being attacked in a parking garage, on public transport, or at an ATM can prepare you for real-life encounters. These drills should include environmental awareness, decision-making under pressure, and physical techniques. By simulating realistic situations, you can develop a more instinctive and effective response.

Another critical aspect of urban self-defense is understanding the legal implications of defending yourself. Laws vary widely by location, but it is essential to know the legal boundaries of using force in self-defense. Generally, the use of force must be reasonable and proportionate to the threat. Excessive force can lead to legal consequences, so it's important to understand what is permissible in your area.

Building a network of trusted individuals can enhance your safety in urban environments. Establishing a community of friends, neighbors, and coworkers who look out for each other can provide mutual support and quick assistance if needed. Informing someone of your whereabouts, especially when traveling alone at night or in unfamiliar areas, adds a layer of security. Sharing information about suspicious activities or individuals can also help keep your community safe.

In some situations, de-escalation techniques can prevent physical confrontations. Learning how to communicate calmly and assertively can diffuse tensions before they escalate into violence. Techniques such as maintaining a non-threatening posture, using a calm tone of voice, and acknowledging the other person's perspective can often resolve a conflict peacefully. The ability to de-escalate is a valuable skill that complements physical self-defense techniques.

Public transportation poses unique challenges for self-defense. Crowded buses or subways can be hotspots for pickpockets and other criminals. When using public transport, keep your belongings secure and in sight. Avoid isolated areas of stations or stops, and if you feel uncomfortable, move closer to the driver or a populated area. Trust your instincts; if a situation feels wrong, remove yourself from it as quickly as possible.

Urban self-defense also involves preparing for emergencies. Carrying a small first aid kit, knowing basic first aid procedures, and having an emergency contact list can be lifesaving. In the event of an injury, knowing how to treat wounds, perform CPR, or provide other basic medical care can make a significant difference until professional help arrives.

Adaptability is a key trait in urban self-defense. Cities are dynamic environments where threats can come from multiple directions and change rapidly. Being able to think on your feet, improvise with available resources, and adapt your strategies to different situations is crucial. This flexibility ensures that you can respond effectively to a wide range of threats.

Ultimately, urban self-defense is about creating a mindset of preparedness and resilience. By staying aware, projecting confidence, learning physical techniques, and understanding the legal and social aspects of self-defense, you can navigate urban environments with greater safety and assurance. Remember, the goal is not to live in fear but to empower yourself with the knowledge and skills needed to protect yourself and those around you. With practice and vigilance, you can transform urban living into a safer and more secure experience.

Communication and Information Gathering in the City

Cities are vibrant hubs of activity, where communication and information gathering play crucial roles in navigating the urban landscape. Whether you're a resident, a visitor, or someone dealing with an emergency, effective communication and the ability to gather accurate information can significantly impact your safety, productivity, and overall experience. This chapter explores practical strategies for enhancing your communication skills and gathering reliable information in the city, emphasizing the use of technology, social networks, and situational awareness.

Imagine stepping into a bustling city for the first time. The streets are teeming with people, vehicles zip by, and the air buzzes with the sounds of urban life. In such a dynamic environment, clear and efficient communication is vital. One of the fundamental aspects of urban communication is understanding and utilizing the various modes of communication available.

Mobile phones are indispensable tools for urban communication. They are not just for voice calls and text messages; smartphones offer a plethora of apps designed to facilitate communication. Messaging apps like WhatsApp, Signal, and Telegram allow for instant messaging, voice calls, and video calls over the internet. These apps often include group chat features, making it easier to coordinate with multiple people simultaneously.

Email remains a crucial communication tool, especially for professional and formal interactions. Ensure that your email setup is efficient by organizing your inbox, creating folders for different types of correspondence, and using filters to prioritize important messages. Email apps on smartphones can sync with your desktop, allowing seamless communication across devices.

Social media platforms are also powerful tools for communication and information gathering. Twitter, for instance, is a valuable resource for real-time updates on traffic, public transportation, and local events. Follow local news outlets, city officials, and community groups to stay informed about what's happening in your area. Facebook groups can connect you with local communities, providing a platform for sharing information, asking for recommendations, and organizing events.

However, with the vast amount of information available online, it's crucial to verify the credibility of sources. Misinformation can spread quickly, especially on social media. Cross-check important information with reputable news sources or official announcements. Be cautious of sensational headlines and verify facts before sharing them.

In an urban setting, face-to-face communication remains essential. Whether you're asking for directions, dealing with a service provider, or interacting with neighbors, effective interpersonal communication skills can make a significant difference. Practice active listening, which involves paying full attention to the speaker, acknowledging their message, and responding thoughtfully. This not only helps in understanding the information being conveyed but also builds rapport and trust.

Nonverbal communication, such as body language and facial expressions, plays a significant role in face-to-face interactions. Maintain eye contact, use open body language, and be mindful of your facial expressions to convey confidence and attentiveness. In multicultural urban environments, being aware of cultural differences in nonverbal communication can prevent misunderstandings and foster positive interactions.

Navigating the city efficiently requires gathering accurate information about your surroundings. Maps and navigation apps like Google Maps, Waze, and Apple Maps are invaluable for this purpose. These apps provide real-time traffic updates, public transportation schedules, and alternate routes. Familiarize yourself with their features, such as offline maps, to ensure you can navigate even without an internet connection.

Public transportation systems are the lifelines of many cities. Understanding how to use them effectively can save time and reduce stress. Most cities have transportation apps that provide schedules, route maps, and service alerts for buses, trains, and subways. Plan your trips in advance and stay updated on any changes or delays. If you're new to the city, don't hesitate to ask locals or transit staff for help.

In addition to digital tools, traditional methods of information gathering are still valuable. Local newspapers, magazines, and community bulletin boards can provide insights into city events, cultural activities, and public announcements. Libraries often serve as information hubs, offering resources on local history, services, and community programs.

Building a personal network in the city can greatly enhance your ability to gather information. Establish connections with neighbors, coworkers, and local business owners. These relationships can provide you with firsthand information about the area, recommendations for services, and updates on local events. Attend community meetings, events, and social gatherings to expand your network and stay engaged with the local community.

In emergencies, effective communication and information gathering become even more critical. Knowing how to contact emergency services, such as police, fire departments, and medical assistance, is essential. Save important numbers in your phone and know the locations of nearby hospitals, police stations, and fire stations.

Emergency alert systems, such as text message alerts and weather apps, can provide timely warnings about natural disasters, severe weather, or other emergencies. Subscribe to local alert systems and stay informed about potential threats. During an emergency, clear and concise communication can save lives. Follow official instructions, share reliable information with others, and check on vulnerable individuals in your community.

Language barriers can pose challenges in urban communication. Learning basic phrases in the predominant language of the city can facilitate interactions and show respect for the local culture. Translation apps and services like Google Translate can bridge language gaps, providing real-time translation for text and speech. In multicultural cities, being open to learning about different cultures and languages can enrich your experience and improve communication.

Staying informed about city regulations and services is also crucial. Many cities have official websites and apps that provide information on public services, local laws, and community resources. Familiarize yourself with these platforms to access information on topics such as waste disposal, parking regulations, public health services, and community programs.

Personal safety is a key consideration in urban communication and information gathering. Share your plans with trusted individuals, especially when exploring unfamiliar areas or attending events. Use location-sharing features on your phone to let someone know your whereabouts. In potentially unsafe situations, trust your instincts and prioritize your safety.

Effective communication and information gathering in the city require a combination of digital tools, interpersonal skills, and situational awareness. By leveraging technology, building personal networks, and staying informed about your surroundings, you can navigate urban environments with confidence and ease. Remember, the key to thriving in the city lies in your ability to connect with others, access reliable information, and adapt to the ever-changing urban landscape.